SHINY FRIENDS SUPER SQUAD

Starr of the Show

1.

by

Leigh Reagan Alley

Illustrated by

Mark Nathan Hurry

Piggy bank PRESS MAINE

For my Shiny Fam Super Squad . . .
my personal team of daydream believers . . .
AJ, Nathan & Brenna.
~LRA

For my loving family, Naomi, Lily, Ruby, and Tasha.
Thank you David Hails, Sarah Claydon, Laura Sedgwick,
and Phil Wright for your wisdom.
~MNH

First Edition 2023

Piggy Bank Press and the colophon are trademarks of Piggy Bank Press.
www.piggybankpress.com

Book design by Piggy Bank Press
Cover design by Piggy Bank Press

ISBN 979-8-218-24596-2 (paperback) ★ ISBN 979-8-218-24595-5 (ebook)

Table of Contents

SUNNY
STARR

Chapter One
Secrets & Lies

Sunny insists that the best thing a person can be is honest. She means it, too.

Example: in the third grade, she knocked Miss Prim's favorite teacup off the corner of her desk by accident, smashing it into a dozen pretty pieces.

She swept it up and told the truth without hesitation, though no one else had been there to see it break. In the end, Miss Prim had made a mosaic from the fragments. All's well that ends well and all that.

Sunny says doing the right thing when no one is looking is the definition of integrity. She's a walking dictionary. That's why everyone says she's the definition of a nerd. Everyone except for me, of course. I'd never say that about my best friend.

Sunny's motto was ringing in my ears as she carried her lunch tray past the cool girls pawing at my backpack. She shot me a confused look. To those girls, we were typically vapor. Attention from them wasn't just rare. It was nonexistent.

My backpack was Sunny's creation. She had deep-cleaned a birdseed sack and attached the straps from an old pair of overalls to it. She had used a butterfly-shaped clasp for its closure because butterflies were her thing. It was awesome.

Even the cool girls thought so, which is why I said I had made it myself when they asked if I had, even though Sunny had made it for my birthday.

It wasn't a lie, exactly. Not in the way that *intentional* lies are lies. Sunny and I had been planning our design collaboration, called Upcycle Everything, for weeks. The backpack was the sort of thing we had talked about doing together. Sunny just . . . did it first.

In addition to being a walking dictionary, like her professor mom, Sunny is a maker, just like her inventor dad. Her dad had made loads from his most famous invention: a microwave sock dryer. Get it? Loads? Laundry? Sometimes I crack myself up.

I wasn't cracking myself up now, obviously, caught in the middle of a . . . fib . . . with Sunny staring laser beams directly into my heart.

The laser beams made it hard to concentrate on what Courtney was saying.

I only caught little snatches of it . . . *go green* . . . *all the rage*. Before I knew it, I was agreeing

to take orders for trash-to-treasure handbags and clutches for Fifth Grade Family Night, which was an annual dinner event that happened just before Sixth Grade Fly-Up. The event began the official countdown to middle school. We couldn't wait to move up and move on.

"I'll spread the word!" said Courtney, trying on the backpack, tossing her shiny blond hair over her shoulder with a swish. "What do you call them?"

I was still looking at Sunny who had stopped looking at me and was instead studying the glob of mashed potatoes and gravy on her tray. Beside her was the empty seat where I should have been.

"Er . . ." I wracked my brain, trying to keep my voice down and sound casual. "Starrdust Bags. You know, with two R's? Like my name."

"Starrdust Bags!" Courtney exclaimed. She wiggled the backpack off her shoulders and handed it to me. "Catchy!"

Sunny rose quickly and rushed to dump her tray. She hadn't even taken a bite of the meatloaf. Her favorite.

My heart sank to my toes.

"You may not know it yet," Kelsey said, "but Courtney just made you an *actual* star, just like you've always dreamed. Courtney just made you the Next Big Thing."

Courtney Crombie decided what was cool at Cooper Elementary. If she said I was big, I was big. Like I'd always wanted to be. But watching Sunny go, I somehow felt smaller than ever.

Chapter Two
Talking Trash

My belly was a rollercoaster of emotions, and I was one loop-de-loop away from The Big Barf. The absolute nerve of Starr, taking the credit for my design! And the hypocrisy! Starr had always said being a Crombie Zombie would be a fate worse than death.

That was her name for Courtney's crowd. Crombie Zombies. What did she want to do now? Let them make her one of them? That was the definition of hypocrisy!

My hunger wasn't helping the circus ride in my stomach. My dad had left for the city the night before to sell one of his inventions on the Shop From Home Network, so our elderly neighbor, Mrs. Wallace, had come to stay the night with me. My dad had said there was cereal in the cupboard for breakfast, and there was, but our milk had gone sour. Mrs. Wallace offered to go to her house to fetch some, but I said I'd be fine with a granola bar. I had been looking forward to Meatloaf Day all morning, until the Crombie Zombies started feeding on Starr's brain.

A sudden and terrible realization hit me. I could feel the color drain from my face. Our art teacher, Miss Heart, must have noticed, too. She was a big noticer of color.

"OK there, Sun?"

I shook my head. "Not OK," I said, clutching my belly and getting to my feet, about to barf for real. "I threw my aligners away in the trash at lunch!" How would I ever find my invisible braces in a dumpster?

"Go," she said, tilting her forehead toward the classroom door. "Maybe Starr can help. She's out there collecting materials for an upcycling project before everything goes to sort at the transfer station."

Just when I thought my day couldn't get any better.

When I rounded the corner of the teachers' parking lot where the dumpster was parked, Starr was pawing around in it through its sliding side door. Courtney and Kelsey were looking on from a distance.

Scattered on the ground beside the massive bin were the spoils of Starr's search so far: an animal cracker box, a toffee popcorn packet, an egg carton, a butter cookie tin, various chip bags, and an empty tub of marshmallow creme. I hoped the set of my jaw gave the impression that I was the definition of irritation and not of jealousy. That marshmallow tub would have been *so much fun* to upcycle.

"Excuse me," I said, clearing my throat. At that moment I'd rather have faced my dad about my missing braces than asked for help from the Crombie Zombies, not that I had much choice. "Has anyone seen my aligners?"

"Ew!" said Courtney. "So gross!" She shook all over like I'd given her a wet willy.

"Like from your actual *mouth*?" said Kelsey, faking a gag. "Mega gross."

Starr didn't stop her digging. I couldn't tell if that was because she didn't care how I was being spoken to or because she was so absorbed with her incredible dumpster finds.

"Why are you so dramatic?" I muttered. It was one of our biggest complaints about the Crombie Zombies.

"Dramatic?" Courtney put both hands on her hips. "Pretty ironic coming from the child star."

I took a sharp breath in and held it. I could feel my blood surging to my freckled cheeks, blending together with my hair into the color I always am when I'm angry: RED.

"Yeah," said Kelsey, crossing her arms in front of her chest and standing as tall as she could. "Pretty rich coming from Little Miss Krunch Klusters herself."

That got Starr's attention. No matter where I go, people still recognize me from that commercial. The dimples, the freckles, the flaming red hair. There is no forgetting I'm *that* kid. I didn't speak a single line. I didn't have to. My job was to take a bite of the competition's cereal--a cereal the Krunch Klusters people had sprinkled with salt. The camera crew captured my pucker-mouthed revulsion in a single, perfect take. My face and my TV family said it all: "Sunny hates it!" At the end of the commercial, I'm smacking happily on a handful of Krunch Klusters, the cereal that the voiceover said Sunnys prefer, six to one.

For the second time that day, Starr watched me go, and she didn't say a word to stop me. *Some best friend,* I thought. For all I cared, my braces could stay lost forever.

Chapter Three

One, Two, Three: Switch

I called Sunny twice after dinner. The first time, her dad said that she was washing

her hair. The second time, he said that she was busy cleaning the bathroom. But she wasn't. I know because we're next-door neighbors, and I could see *with my own actual eyes* that she was doing no such things.

What she actually *was* doing was ripping up "Freckles," the song I'd written for her tenth birthday and performed for her on my ukulele. I'd had my mom get the lyrics blown up to poster size and framed. Now the song was in a dozen pieces like that broken teacup of Miss Prim's, but these pieces weren't pretty. Sunny crumpled them and tossed them straight into her wastebasket.

Oof.

BE
AMAZING
BE
AWESOME
BE
BRAVE
most of all
BE
YOU

As though she knew I was watching, Sunny crossed to her window and brushed her hands together as if to say she was done with an unpleasant task and with me, too. She snapped her blinds closed even though we always slept with them open in case one of us had to signal the other in the middle of the night with some important flashlight message.

I wondered what words were swirling around in that wordy, red head of hers. I doubted any were 'best' or 'friend.'

★ ★ ★

The next morning, Sunny dodged me for our entire first three periods. When I asked to borrow something to write with in math, she had her tablemate, Sarah, tell me she didn't have an extra, even though I could see her feather pen peeking *very plainly* from the pocket of her backpack. She had always let me use her favorite pink pen. Her Thinking Pen.

The one she jotted down all her newspaper story ideas with.

Always until now, apparently.

When I asked her to help me with a verb conjugation in Spanish, she asked Sarah to tell me to conjugate it my own stupid self. And when I asked if I could have a look at her plot pyramid in English, she tucked it into her binder without a word, like I hadn't even spoken. Like I didn't exist at all.

Fourth period meant science. That would set us right. We had the science fair coming up and ours was going to be the best project Cooper Elementary had ever seen. It was blue-ribbon stuff, for sure. We were going to build a saltwater circuit to power a lightbulb for emergency use and show other people how to make their own. It was going to be epic. It was going to be enlightening. Literally.

Or so I had thought. All of that changed when Sunny's hand went up.

"I want to switch science partners," she blurted, all in one breath, looking at me with side-eyes she didn't seem to care if I noticed.

Our science teacher, Mr. Quark, studied her with his mouth hung open, like she was some new strain of foot fungus about to invade all of our toenails. The inseparable Starr and Sunny, indivisible no more? Unbelievable. At least that's what his gaping mouth seemed to say. Starr without Sunny was like peanut butter without jelly. Ketchup without mustard. Cookie without milk.

"It's a little late for that, Scientist Sunny," tutted Mr. Quark, shaking his head and smoothing his wacky, science-themed necktie. "Everyone is paired like electrons. The science fair is just around the corner."

Yes! Mr. Quark was being cool. So cool. He was saving my day and my friendship both.

"I understand," Sunny said. But then things went from cool to deep-freeze. "In that case, we'll have to work solo."

"If you two are having trouble collaborating, then I suppose . . ." Mr. Quark's voice trailed off. He studied my face like I was an experiment and observed it for any data to indicate my disagreement. I only shrugged.

If Sunny didn't want to be my partner anymore, what could I say?

Super-oof. In a single period, I'd gone from emergency light to alone in the dark.

Chapter Four
All Ears

For someone who had been basically invisible a few days ago, Starr was getting

a whole lot of everyone's attention. Every morning after homeroom bell and every day before dismissal, the all-call button on the school intercom belonged to her. Her voice was everywhere, and everyone was all ears. It was probably rude to cover mine whenever she came over the airwaves, but I couldn't pretend Cooper Elementary's newest idol wasn't a complete phony.

"Wear green, think green, live green!" she was proclaiming in this bizarre, perky voice that sounded nothing like her real one. "Walk the green carpet like a celeb at the Fifth Grade Family Night one week from Friday! And don't forget to snag your Starrdust Bags for the big event!" It was as though every time she opened her mouth, it was actually

Courtney talking. I'd never pictured Starr as a puppet. Least of all Courtney's.

If it sounds like I was bitter, that's because I was the *definition* of bitter.

Later, when I told my dad about it, he said that I should give Starr a break. That she'd always said she had been lonely as an "only." I didn't have any siblings, either, but you didn't see me stealing people's ideas to get attention. I said so to Dad. But Dad said that Starr's needs and mine might be different. Ugh. Sometimes I hated when my dad had a point.

I didn't stop thinking about his point through the rest of dinner. Or through the sitcom we watched together afterward. Or through laying out my school clothes for the next morning. Or through brushing my teeth and turning out the light.

I had a strange feeling in the pit of my stomach. It was a feeling I couldn't ignore. Starr and I were best friends. We'd been best friends basically from birth. If I wasn't lonely because I had her, why was she so lonely when she had me?

★ ★ ★

I was lost in that thought again the next day at school, fidgeting with my feathery Thinking Pen, when my name crackled over the intercom: *Sunny Morgan, report to the office. Sunny Morgan.*

I glanced at the clock and gathered my things into my knapsack. By the time I got to the office, it would be almost time for the bus home.

I gave Mr. Stevens a sheepish nod on my way past his standing desk. He gave me a disapproving look over the top of his glasses but didn't say a word. I should've been working on a story for the school paper instead of stuck in a cloud, contemplating why my friendship wasn't enough for Starr. The paper was due out in just two days. I'd been assigned to interview Starr as a feature for that week's *Cooper Chronicle*, but that wasn't happening. She had stuck a four-word note in my locker at the first of the week: "The interview is off." At least we could agree on something.

When I arrived at the office, the administrative assistant, Ms. Lottie, handed me a plastic baggie. Her eyes glinted like her glasses chain. "Been looking for these?" she said. My aligners were inside.

Relief washed over me. Somehow my dad hadn't noticed they were missing. I guess undetectable is the definition of invisible. "How did you find them?" I asked, hugging the baggie to my chest.

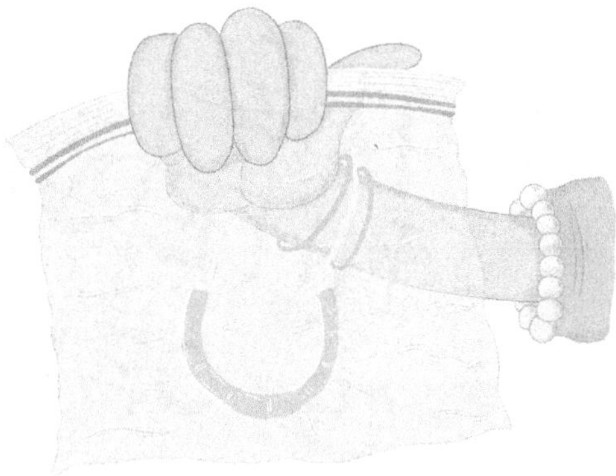

"None of my doing," she said, smiling.

"But . . . who? *How*?"

"The Tooth Fairy, I guess." Her eyes were all mischief, crinkled at the corners. The final bell rang, and she shooed her hands in the direction of the lobby. "Scoot!"

I had a sneaking suspicion that this particular Tooth Fairy had a jet-black choppy bob, a naturally-straight smile, and a birdseed sack backpack, compliments of me. If this was Starr's way of apologizing, I was listening.

Chapter Five
Making the Headlines

At the start of Thursday morning, I was walking on air. I'd taken thirty orders for

Starrdust Bags. I'd managed to rescue Sunny's aligners. I'd been invited to co-host a show for Cooper Radio, WCOO. The club adviser, Ms. Singh, said I had a real voice for it. She said I could bring my ukulele to perform my original songs on air and everything! I could pinch myself. Starr was on the rise. I could feel it.

But by the end of Thursday morning, I was walking on eggshells. In ELA, the rumor whispered up and down the aisles was that I was going to be on the front page of the *Chronicle* the next morning, whether I liked the idea or not.

A headline had been leaked among some of the kids: Starr Solomon Has a Secret!

"Ooh, I wonder what that's about," whispered Courtney from behind me. "Juicy!"

My belly flip-flopped. Hopefully the "secret" was a positive one, not Sunny's revenge for the stolen idea and the canceled interview. I thought I'd be doing her a favor, sparing her from having to speak to me. She seemed to be pretty bent on avoiding it.

I ripped a page from my notebook and took out a permanent marker. *I can't believe you'd do this to me,* I wrote. *It's like I never knew you at all!* I underlined every word twice, so she could see how serious I was.

I crumpled the lined paper into a tight wad and tossed it toward Sunny. She jumped as it landed on her desktop. It had been a while since I'd thrown a note at her. She had clearly stopped expecting them.

Sunny studied the wad for a moment, then she smoothed back a red curl from her forehead and unfolded it.

As soon as Sunny read the underlined words, I could see her ears turn scarlet. She. Was. Furious.

She almost toppled her chair, she got up from it so roughly. She turned and pointed a shaky finger at me.

"It's like YOU never knew ME at all?" She re-crumpled the note and hurled it onto my desk. "You, Starr Solomon, are the definition of nerve!"

Miss Garner's head snapped up. "Do I need to send you to the principal's office, Sunny?" she asked sternly, straightening her glasses. She'd never seen an outburst like that from Sunny before. Nobody had.

"No," said Sunny. "I'll send myself. I could use some time in the Cool-Down Corner." She shoved her things into her backpack, slung the backpack onto her shoulder, and shot me a disgusted look as she passed.

"Yow!" Courtney said to me. "Your best friend is a touchy one!"

"EX-best friend!" Sunny said, pretending to underline the words as she spoke them. She didn't miss a beat on her way out the door.

Chapter Six
Exposed

Friday in the hallway before the first bell, everyone was already buzzing. Starr had

been exposed--anonymously and vaguely, but brutally--on the front page of the *Cooper*

Chronicle. I hid in the back office of the newsroom to read the feature in private.

COOPER
Chronicle

☆ STARR SOLOMON HAS A SECRET ☆

If you had no idea who Starr Solomon was until recently, you weren't alone. But suddenly the whole school is abuzz because of this new Queen Bee. Starr is setting trends and making friends.

Great, right?

Wrong!

The problem, fellow Cooper Comets, is that Starr is a fake and a fraud. Remember her slogan, "Think green! Live green!"? More like, *Think yellow!*

Live yellow! Starr Solomon is a complete coward. She has been passing off other people's ideas as her own, and she is too yellow-bellied to admit it.

If you value honesty, send a message to Starr Solomon, and boycott Starrdust Bags.

I was Assistant Editor. How had this story sneaked past me? Remembering all the cool-off time I'd spent outside Principal Crowley's office the day before, I had to admit I had a vague idea of how I had missed it. I had seriously dropped the ball on my newspaper responsibilities.

My head said Starr had brought this on herself and deserved it, but my heart said nobody did. I glanced at the clock.

7:55 AM. Starr's parents always dropped her off at ten minutes 'til eight. With luck, she'd gone straight to her locker and not seen the Friday paper.

I tucked my copy of the *Chronicle* under my arm. If I hurried, I thought, maybe I could catch her and soften the blow somehow.

As I was reaching for the knob, the door jerked open, and in stepped Starr, her eyes wet with tears and flashing with anger. Courtney and Kelsey were behind her, their arms folded across their chests. Courtney's smirk said they hadn't come for a friendly chat.

"How could you?" Starr demanded. "I get that you're upset. I've tried to make it up to you." She shook a copy of the *Chronicle* in my face. "This is what I get?" she sobbed. "I'm a fake and a fraud and the fifth graders should boycott my bags? You couldn't say it to my face, so you said it to our entire school?"

I felt for her. I did. But there she was blaming me again for something I didn't do. As tears filled my own eyes, I pushed past Starr, out of the back office and into the larger newsroom. Kids reporting to homeroom had heard Starr's every word and assumed I was the anonymous author.

"Oh, boo-hoo, Baby Krunch Klusters," Courtney hissed. "It must really bother you to be standing in the background while Starr gets some of the spotlight."

A spotlight was the last thing I'd ever wanted, and Starr knew that. It was Starr who wanted to be a celebrity. I wanted to be invisible. Anonymous.

All the same, Starr didn't correct her. How was I supposed to defend myself? I couldn't even formulate a thought with so many of our classmates there, watching. It was the definition of a scene.

"Ignore her," Courtney told Starr, making an ugly face at me. "She's a hater."

How was this *happening*? How had this turned around on *me*?

From somewhere behind me, someone crooned softly, mockingly, "Sunny hates it!"

Everyone laughed. Even Starr, through her tears.

It wasn't as though it was the first time I'd heard it, but throughout our growing up, whenever someone had mocked me with that cereal tagline in front of Starr, she had somehow made the whole world feel OK. She could shoot her disapproving laser eyes straight through anyone. That was the thing about Starr. She never went looking for arguments, but she didn't back down when the cause was right.

I turned to scan the crowd of faces, to find out who my real friends were. Tyler Sterling had been my locker neighbor since third grade. Tyler wasn't laughing. *He was the only one not laughing*. And he shot me a sympathetic look.

Mr. Stevens came in at the last bell, ready to take attendance. "Where do you belong, Sunny?" he said, surprised to see me there and at the obvious center of everyone's attention.

"No place, it feels like."

I shouldered my bag and plodded toward the door. Some start to Friday: humiliated and late for homeroom.

Chapter Seven

Damage Control

At lunchtime, I was huddled talking with Courtney and the crew at the back of the

cafetorium. The topic? How to get a handle on things before the piece in the paper had a chance to derail

THE event of the season. The solution according to Courtney? A weekend social media blitz. Q&A with the creator of Starrdust Bags. Before-and-afters of the raw materials and the rad outcomes. A giveaway.

I hadn't made a single bag yet, but that didn't seem like such a big deal. The process would be quick . . . probably. How long could thirty bags take? A couple of hours? *No problem.*

Courtney passed a bag of cheese curls my way. I hated cheese curls. Hated how the cheese powder stained my fingertips orange and stuck in the crevices of my molars. They were Courtney's favorite food, though, so I helped myself to a handful.

Friday was Pizza Day. Not so very long ago, I'd have been sitting beside Sunny as always, putting her picked-off pepperonis onto my slice, and we'd have been making epic plans for our weekend.

Thinking about it, I couldn't help glancing over. When I did, I didn't like what I saw. Tyler Sterling was sitting in my spot. Well, what *had been* my spot. Granted, I hadn't used it in a while.

Seeing my usual seat empty all these days had hurt. But seeing it filled with Tyler hurt worse. I noticed how he hadn't laughed at the Krunch Klusters line when everyone else had.

Watching the way Sunny smiled at him, it was me who wasn't laughing.

Courtney snapped her orange fingers in front of my face. "Starr! Earth to Starr!"

"What?" I said, frowning to let her know I didn't appreciate being *literally* snapped at.

"Who are you going to walk the green carpet with at Family Night?" Courtney asked, looking impatient.

I knew I was supposed to say I planned to walk it with her and Kelsey, but my heart wasn't in it.

I took another look at Sunny and Tyler, wondering if he was asking her the same question Courtney had just asked me.

Things had always been Starr *plus* Sunny. Pizza Fridays . . . Sunday Fundays . . . movie matinees . . . special school events. Now there were just Starr *and* Sunny, two solo-flying free agents. Nothing was a given anymore.

The memory of Sunny's betrayal of me in the *Chronicle* flooded back and washed away all of the other feelings floating around inside my heart.

"Not Sunny," I said, finally. And that was perfectly fine with me.

Chapter Eight
So. Not. OK.

A giant gang of kids crammed around a locker trying to look casual is almost

never a good sign. It's basically the definition of a bad omen. One you can spot from the other end of the hallway, like a black cat, or a broken mirror, or a ladder you're not supposed to walk under, or a crack you're not supposed to step on.

I was tempted to leave my coat and backpack in my locker for the weekend to avoid whatever drama was awaiting me, but it was chilly outside, and I had a Spanish test to study for.

As I approached the group it sort of split in half and opened for me like those double doors you see on restaurant kitchens.

When the kids parted, I could see immediately what the fuss was all about. Someone had printed off a screen grab from my Krunch Klusters commercial and taped it to my locker door. In the photo, my little face was twisted up in revulsion. Starr's backpack had been pasted in place of the cereal bowl. "Sunny hates it!" was scribbled at the bottom in permanent marker.

Sunny MADE it! I screamed inside my head as I tore off the photo, crumpled it, and dialed my locker combination. *And Sunny didn't write that stupid article!*

When my locker swung open, hundreds of photocopies slid from it like an avalanche and pooled around my ankles. Someone had taken time to fold them all in half and stuff them through my locker vents.

"Really classy," I muttered. To keep from crying, in my head I started to spell the longest word in the Oxford English Dictionary:

pneumonoultramicroscopicsilicovolcanoconiosis.

It's a factitious word for a chronic lung disease. I could imagine what it must be like to have that. I hadn't taken a good, deep breath in forever. Or, in other words, in all the time that I had been at odds with Starr.

I wondered what Starr would say, seeing this. Then it occurred to me that Starr probably had helped to pull the prank. The thought made me want to fold in half and stuff myself inside my locker.

* * *

Both my bus ride home and my dinner were lonelier than I thought I could stand. Dad was in the city again, promoting his latest invention: an umbrella that rains ice water on you in hot weather. He calls it the TripDrip because it's perfect for trips to the beach, the carnival, the park, and the playground. Personally, I thought it was pretty zany. Dad said that it also was

pretty obvious, which is what the best inventions always seem . . . *after* they've been invented.

I was loading the dishwasher and wishing I could invent a teleportation device when the phone rang. It was Mum, which was quite coincidental since I'd been wishing I could teleport to her and not have to wait for school vacation to go visit her on her sabbatical in London.

I'd been about to tell her about our mind-bending jinx when she pulled in a deep breath and puffed it back out again. I didn't like the sound of it. Not a little bit.

"Peaches," she said, "I'm just going to say something before I lose my nerve. Rip the bandaid and all that."

"OK," I said, lamely. I wasn't a rocket scientist like she was, but I could tell from experience where this was headed.

"It's not going to work, I'm afraid. The trip, I mean."

All the breath went out of my lungs like a punctured balloon

"OK," I said, lamely.

"It's just that I have quite a lot to do at the moment--research, you know--and a lot of late nights coming up."

"OK," I said, lamely.

"You understand, don't you, Darling? We'll reschedule it soon, I promise."

"OK," I said, lamely.

"Can't you say something else? You're sounding a bit like a broken record."

"OK," I said, lamely.

I was anything but OK.

My parents had been divorced since I was three. They were already divorcing when a casting director spotted me in the grocery store and approached my mom about the Krunch Klusters commercial. I couldn't even remember a time when we had lived together as a family. Looking around my too-quiet, two-story house at the end of the cul-de-sac, I couldn't imagine one, either.

It took a few minutes for me to realize that my mother was still talking. "I love you, Pumpkin," she concluded. "I'll call you in a couple of days. OK?"

"OK," I said, lamely.

She hung up before I could manage to say that I loved her, too.

Later that evening, Dad came home full of excitement. I had watched his TripDrip sell out while he was still live on air.

"It feels good to be in demand!" he said, loading the dishwasher while I ate the huge caramel apple he'd brought to me from one of his fellow Shop From Home Network sellers.

I was happy for him, but I couldn't help feeling gloomy about canceled visits, canceled friendships, and canceled plans.

"I wouldn't know," I said, throwing the caramel apple stick in the trash.

★ ★ ★

Saturday morning had brought exactly as much boredom as I imagined it would. There was nothing good on TV. There was no one to play with. I'd read every book on my shelves twice before. Except for a lightbulb and the aluminum foil I knew I could find in my kitchen cupboards, I had already gathered my materials for the science fair and had already made the how-to poster. I had absolutely nothing to do. But all the same, I couldn't spend my entire day sulking. That would be the definition of pathetic.

It was time to think.

I pulled my favorite Thinking Pen from my backpack and fiddled with the soft, pink feather on its end.

I replayed the awfulness of my rift with Starr in my mind, wondering if she was feeling miserable, too. We had never had a problem communicating, but it felt nearly impossible now.

I took out a sheet of notepaper. It had little stars sprinkled across it. Starr's symbol, she had always told me . . . because someday, like her name said, she would be one. My eyes wandered to the spot above my bed where a birthday song Starr had written me had hung before I'd torn it up.

Oh, Freckles, don't you see

You're butterflies and stars to me?

How had things gotten so jumbled?

I put my pen to the notepaper and tried to pour what I was feeling onto the page:

Dear Starr,

There were so many words I wanted to say, but I knew I'd never find the right ones to explain my sadness, my anger, or my loneliness. Finally, I just wrote, *I miss you. Love, Sunny*

I tucked the piece of notepaper away in my desk and fluffed the feather of my Thinking Pen some more. All morning I had tried to ignore my curiosity about what Starr might be doing. My dad had figured out that Starr and I'd had a rift. He suggested that I bake some of my “famous” cupcakes and invite Starr over to patch things up if possible. Maybe it wasn’t such a bad idea . . .

I tiptoed over to my window to peek through the blinds. If she was out in her yard, I told myself, I’d holler and ask her to come make the famous cupcakes with me. Cupcakes with double frosting, double sprinkles, and double jelly filling.

Starr was in her yard, all right, standing at a folding table she’d set up to accommodate a gigantic pile of the product packaging she intended to upcycle into bags. The Crombie Zombies were there, filming what I guessed was an interview, their phones up to catch Starr’s every word.

It was ironic to watch, since neither Starr nor I were allowed to have any of the smartphone apps they probably were planning to upload the footage to. The Zombies had made fun of us not even two months before because we "bedwetters" weren't on any social media, so, by their logic, what was the point of our even having phones?

If I were a cartoon, steam would have been spouting from my ears. I took a deep breath and held it. There she was making OUR dream HER reality. I needed to find a way to cool down and get back into my "upstairs brain," the way our tween issues counselor had taught our class to do in assembly on our first day of fifth grade.

If I started making more decisions with my upstairs brain, maybe I'd feel better about the situation I didn't like but couldn't change.

I took the note to Starr back out of my desk drawer and flipped the page over. On it, I wrote,

To-Do:

★ Bake Dad Some Cupcakes

★ Send Mum a Letter

★ Try Something New

At that moment, Dad came into my bedroom, jangling his car keys, asking if I felt like ice cream for lunch (uh, *yes*!).

Suddenly, I had an idea.

"Dad," I said, "I feel some inspiration coming on."

"Inspiration," my dad whispered, and I could practically see the little inventor-gears turning in his head. "I like it!"

* * *

The inside of Moving Stationery was magical. At least Starr and I had always said so. It was so much more than a stationery store. In addition to cute notepads and handmade papers, there were paints, clays, unfinished wood projects, and the supplies for just about every kind of craft imaginable.

So many of my Starr memories had their start at Moving Stationery. Our tie-dye phase. Our knitting phase. Our stained glass phase. Our fairy garden phase. (OK, maybe that hadn't been a phase. We both still loved our fairy gardens. Or I did, at least. I couldn't really guess what Starr might love anymore. Case in point: since when did Starr Solomon eat cheese curls? I mean, *ew*!)

At the back corner of the store were the how-to books. I could learn to crochet. That would be fun. Or take up calligraphy?

Then I saw it: *Simple Green Crafts, Step by Step*. I slipped the book from the shelf and thumbed through it. With patience and practice, I knew I could learn to make the beautiful things inside, and in some small way, help people and the planet . . . and something I saw on page 13 gave me a pretty good idea of where to start.

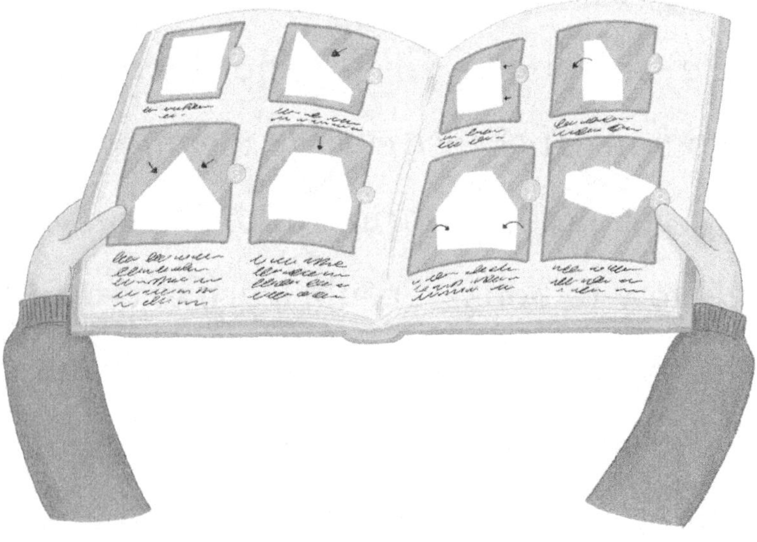

Chapter Nine
Trash to Treasure

Come lunchtime at half-past 11:00 Monday, I was half-past exhausted. The weekend had been a lot less productive and a whole lot tougher than I had thought it would be. Originally,

Courtney and Kelsey had planned to be with me all of Friday afternoon and Saturday, lending a hand and "documenting the creative process."

All that meant was that they wanted to make a Starrdust Bags channel and post a bunch of stuff on a bunch of social platforms I've been absolutely forbidden to join. When it turned out that I wasn't really in favor of that idea, they bailed. In the trash-to-treasure equation, they said, they were *wayyyyy* more interested in the treasure than the trash. Oof.

I did manage to make ten bags, but with twenty bags to go, and school all week--not to mention a science fair I hadn't prepared for!--the chances of filling all of the orders seemed pretty unlikely.

Courtney and Kelsey had made it sound so cool to have orders up to my eyeballs. And it was. At first. Up until my eyeballs couldn't see any light at the end of the bag-making tunnel.

I was internally lamenting all of it as I spun my locker combination to stash my books when out fluttered a slip of paper that made my heart sink the way Sunny's probably had when all of the photocopies

Courtney and Kelsey had made avalanched down:

Bad news, Starr. It was Piper who wrote that scorching burn piece for the paper last week. You stole her idea for the green carpet and didn't give her any credit? Savage!

FYI,

Court -n- Kels

I had wrongly and publicly accused my own best (*ex*-best?) friend of taking our feud to the school paper. And it was true: I really had borrowed the idea for a green carpet from Piper. Double oof.

I had made nothing but missteps and mistakes lately. I thought back to the weekend when I had seen Sunny climb out of her dad's car with a shopping tote from Moving Stationery slung over her shoulder. I had wanted to holler over and ask what she had bought there, but Kelsey and Courtney had been in the middle of interviewing me for their QuickieScoop video loop.

Every loop is only ten seconds long. "Give us the scoop on your bags!" they said.

My response? "Easy! They're fashionable and guilt-free!" Guilt-free. *Guilt. Free.* Talk about false advertising.

Chapter Ten
Warmth & Light

My weekend to-do list had lifted my spirits. My dad had loved the cupcakes.

(This time I'd done double peanut butter frosting with double grape jelly.) My mum had loved the note. (I'd sent lots of photos of what I'd been up to so that we could reconnect, and we had video-chatted for hours after she opened my email.) And I had loved making pretty and useful things from odds and ends I had lying around my house.

Once I started crafting, I couldn't stop! Soon I had made a succulent pot from an old seltzer can, some garden stakes from our mismatched silverware, and a set of refrigerator magnets from a bottle cap collection dad had kept when he was a kid. When Sunday had come to a close, I'd had a beautiful collection

of salvaged and repurposed crafts that made my dad and me smile. But more than that, I'd had a plan--a plan to spread some warmth and light and, in the process, to shoo away the dark cloud that had been hanging over Starr and me once and for all.

* * *

"So, it's pretty easy, you see?" I said, making the last fold and tuck necessary to turn a bioplastic pretzel bag into a repurposed wallet. I paused to take a bite of my sandwich.

Our old fourth grade teacher, Mr. Craft, applauded. That was how Mr. Craft always was: supportive. He had been so excited when my dad had called him on Sunday night with my hope of visiting his classroom with a lunchtime treat and enlisting his students to help make upcycled wallets to give to Starr.

Tyler took a final peek at the instructions on the Smart Whiteboard behind us, finished taping and folding, and showed his to the class. It had been really nice of him to offer to join me to help everyone get their wallets just right.

The fourth graders were all smiles as they finished their pretzels and popcorn and cereal snacks and commenced with folding. The spirit of community service was alive and well at Cooper Elementary.

"Mine's not bad," Tyler said to the fourth graders. "It's not perfect, but it's not bad. And yours doesn't have to be perfect, either."

We started around the room with the help of Mr. Craft, ripping off strips of biodegradable tape and sticking them to the edges of the kids' desks so they would be ready when they needed them. Within five minutes, we had twenty wallets made by twenty kids.

"Remember, Mr. Craft has put these instructions on the homepage for your online classroom," I said. "When you leave today, grab an afterschool snack from the box and make another wallet at home to keep for yourselves or to give to someone you care about."

Mr. Craft collected up the wallets and put a shiny, colorful stack of them into my outstretched hand and Tyler's. "Thank you for coming in today," said Mr. Craft. "It's always nice to connect with your former students in a meaningful way before they move on to middle school. It's good to know your former class is still kind."

I thought about the unkind ways Starr had treated me recently and the unkind ways I had behaved toward her and felt my heart sink.

But then I remembered a shining act of kindness: my found braces. And thought of my own kind act in return: the wallets I hoped would complete Starr's orders for their big debut on the green carpet at Fifth Grade Family Night.

My sinking heart started to rise. "We're going to make you proud, Mr. Craft."

As soon as I said the words, my heart knew they were honest and true. And as I always like to say, that is the best thing a person can be.

Chapter Eleven
Nothing but the Truth

The next day at the start of fourth period, it was time to force the truth into the light. It was the day of the science fair, and even though I had tried my best to stay up late to make a

paper mache volcano the night before, I had fallen asleep atop my newspapers and paste. Talk about a sticky situation.

I raised my hand to come clean, which felt pretty ironic in its own way since I was still covered with dried-on

paste and black smudges from the newsprint.

Mr. Quark looked up from his attendance log and called on me.

"What can I do for you, Starr?"

"Well . . . erm . . ." I wiped at a particularly gross sticky-smudge spot near my wrist. "It's really about what I didn't do for you. It's about my science project."

Around me swirled the whispers I had expected. From what I'd heard, half the fifth grade had commented on the QuickieScoop video, saying I'd never finish the bags or my science project, either. They said the *Cooper Chronicle* had been right: that I was a phony who didn't make good on her promises. From what I'd heard, Courtney and Kelsey hadn't really defended me.

My ears grew almost as red as Sunny's always did when she was mad. But I wasn't mad. I was ashamed. Ashamed by the feeling that I had proven those mean QuickieScoop comments right.

"Go on, Starr," said Mr. Quark, adjusting his wacky-as-ever, science-y necktie.

I could feel some verbal vomit welling up. It was time to blurt out the truth and get it over with. "I don't have a finished project," I said, covering my mouth as if even I couldn't believe what had just come out of it.

"But the fair is tonight," said Mr. Quark. "It's *tonight.*"

"I know," I said, feeling the weight of having disappointed both Mr. Quark and myself. I put my head on my desk.

"All she *means,*" said a familiar voice that made my ears perk, "is that she didn't bring our aluminum foil and lightbulb, Mr. Quark."

I picked my head up off my desk. Sunny Morgan was *lying*? For *me*?

Mr. Quark looked happier than I imagined Newton had looked when the gravity-apple had bonked him on the head.

"So, the two of you are working together after all? I had a feeling you'd sort things out!" He motioned his hands as if to say we should move our seats together.

"Before you say anything," said Sunny, "it isn't a lie. At least it won't be. Bring the bulb and foil tonight. And stop by Miss Heart's room after. Tyler and I have a surprise for you."

My mouth hung open the way Mr. Quark's had the day Sunny had said she wanted to un-partner with me. I was shocked, grateful, and speechless.

Sunny Morgan was a walking dictionary. But she also was the walking, talking definition of a surprise.

I couldn't help but hug her.

Chapter Twelve
Squad Goals

Our science fair project was not as impressive as Starr and I had imagined it

would be so many weeks before. We each earned a white ribbon that said Honorable Mention on it in foil letters . . . but so had everyone else in our class who hadn't won a medal. All in all, our saltwater circuit was the definition of mediocrity.

Somehow that didn't matter so much when Starr walked in and saw the neat little rows of snack-bag wallets spread out atop a table in Miss Heart's room. Starr's eyes glittered like the celestial lights that inspired her name. From where I was standing, I couldn't tell if that was from happiness or tears or both.

She picked up one, turning it over and over again in her hands. "You did this?"

Tyler and I nodded.

"They're so cool!" she went on, admiring them. "They're so pretty!

They're so clever!"

"And they were so easy!" Tyler said. "We had lots of help from Mr. Craft's fourth grade."

I took Starr's free hand and led her to where Miss Heart was sitting with her open laptop. "There's something else we need to show you, too," I said.

On her screen was a logo the fourth graders had worked with Mr. Craft to design. Miss Heart explained how she had digitized it and printed it onto fabric labels that could be glued to every Starrdust Bag.

"That is so neat," Kelsey breathed. I think we all jumped a little. No one had seen her come in.

"Sorry," she said. "I hope I wasn't interrupting. I overheard you from the hall."

"You're not interrupting," I said.

Starr gave me a grateful look, and Kelsey gave me a smile.

"I wanted to help more," Kelsey said to Starr. "With your bags, I mean. What you were doing was so great. Part of me wanted to get messy with you in that dumpster that very first day."

"You could have," Starr said.

"I don't know," Kelsey said, frowning. "It wasn't what people would have expected from me. Besides, it was the kind of thing you and Sunny would typically do. Just the two of you. Together. I kept expecting her to come join you. Nobody wants to be odd one out."

Starr and I exchanged glances. The kind that, between best friends, could say it all. The kind that said the feud that had divided us was definitely over. The kind that said we had never considered whether the friendship that pulled us so close to each other might have pushed away other friends and classmates.

A silence settled over us. But it wasn't the kind of silence that had separated us lately . . . the silence that comes from misunderstandings. It was the kind of silence that said words were unnecessary because at that moment everyone was understanding each other perfectly.

"We're here now," Starr said, finally. "It's not too late for us to do something together."

"Like making more wallets?" Tyler asked. "I have to admit, that was pretty fun. My little brother has made four or five to give to friends since I showed him how."

We all smiled.

"If it's OK with you, I'm retiring from the bag-making business!" Starr said.

It was fine by us. All was well that ended well, but Starrdust Bags had driven us far apart before bringing us together again.

"Oh, no," said Starr, remembering something that made the color go out of her cheeks.

"What's wrong?" said Kelsey.

Starr wrung her hands. "I took payments for those bags. I have *sixty dollars* in sales. Do you think we should give it to the fourth-grade class? They're the ones who made most of them."

"I'm not sure," Tyler said. "Sunny's dad is the one who purchased the materials."

We all looked at each other with our eyebrows raised. There didn't seem to be a clear-cut answer.

We settled at one of Miss Heart's tables. She took a carton of fish-shaped crackers out of the closet by her desk and poured a little pile for us onto one of the coffee filters she kept for use in her art projects.

"So, what should we do with it?" said Kelsey, after we had finished the snack.

"I have an idea!" said Miss Heart, gathering up the coffee filter, wadding it into a ball, and tossing it into the recycling bin next to her desk. "Do good!"

We liked that idea.

"What about starting a club?" I said.

"A kindness club?" offered Starr.

"A kindness club!" we all agreed.

"What will we call it?" Kelsey asked. "It's not too late to get a club advisor and take on some positivity projects before we move up to sixth grade."

"Kindness Club seems too generic," said Tyler. "It's what we do, but it's not *who we are*."

Starr nodded in agreement.

"Do-Gooders?" said Kelsey.

Tyler, Starr, and I groaned jokingly. It was a nice nod to Miss Heart who suggested that we "do good," but it was too corny even for me, Little Miss Krunch Klusters.

The names Caring Crew, Smile Awhile, and Upside Down Frown all got similar reactions.

"It seems like we're stumped," said Tyler. He turned to Miss Heart. "Any ideas?"

"Shiny Friends," she offered. "After its founders."

From the thoughtful looks on their faces, I could tell Kelsey, Starr, and Tyler didn't hate it.

"I don't dislike it," I said, "but don't you think the name should reflect all four of us founders, not just Starr and me?"

"Oh, but it does," said Miss Heart, with a gleam in her eye that said she had seen something we perhaps hadn't. "*Starr* Solomon, *Sunny* Morgan, Kelsey *Gold*, and Tyler *Sterling*. Shiny Friends, every last one."

I had to admit, I loved that.

"Shiny Friends," Starr said, trying the name on. "That's good. But Shiny Friends Super Squad is better."

Leave it to Starr to add her own artistic twist. I laughed out loud, but I had to admit that the name had a ring to it.

"Shiny Friends Super Squad?" I said, putting my hand in like I had seen our basketball teams do in their huddles.

"Shiny Friends Super Squad!" the others agreed, putting their hands atop mine.

Miss Heart cleared her throat. "You know who else has some potential as a Shiny Friend?" she said.

"Who?" we asked in unison.

"Courtney *Luna* Crombie."

This time my groan wasn't fake.

I was the definition of doubt, but maybe in time, the idea would grow on me.

Chapter Thirteen
Starr of the Show

Fifth Grade Family Night was the kind of night that made you pinch yourself to check if you were dreaming.

I gave an interview on Cooper Radio before the green carpet event, explaining that a green carpet wasn't my idea at all. That it was Piper's. It felt good to get the truth out there and to give credit where it was due.

Piper's green carpet was a hit with the fifth graders and our families, and so were Starrdust Bags. I think I could have taken a hundred orders. It was flattering that everyone liked them, but I still got a knot in my belly every time I thought about how such a teensy-seeming lie about my birthday backpack had driven such a gigantic wedge between my best friend and me. Remembering was not a good feeling.

What *was* a good feeling was getting to be the headlining act for Fifth Grade Family Night . . . the Starr of the Show, the posters said. Everyone got to their feet and cheered at the end of my three-song ukulele set. Especially Sunny who had a way of driving my nervous butterflies away with her smile. I finished with the song I wrote for her when she turned ten: "Freckles."

I think after she tore it up, Sunny thought the song was lost for good. But some things are forever . . . like the story about that time in kindergarten when you got caught eating a glue stick . . . or that permanent marker stain you accidentally put on your teacher's dry-erase board . . . or your red-haired best friend and the lyrics she inspired.

Another good feeling was when Shiny Friends Super Squad announced the first of our club-sponsored Squad Goals: a Buddy Bench to sit near the four square and hopscotch games in the playground down on the fourth-grade end of the building. From now on, no one would have to be alone during recess. We put the first $60 toward the project, and the rest of the funding we needed was donated before Fifth Grade Family Night was through.

But for me, the best feeling of the night was that Sunny's mom flew in to surprise her, arriving just in time to see the Shiny Friends Super Squad walk the green carpet together with our matching shades, clutching our matching wallets, making silly faces with our advisors, Miss Heart and Mr. Quark.

On Monday morning, we would be off to our middle school fly-up, but for the moment, our hearts were with our families and friends, and our heads were still in Grade Five.

We were in no rush to leave with so much springtime still ahead and so much good for the Shiny Friends Super Squad still to do at Cooper Elementary School.

And that was the honest truth.

BUDDY BENCH

STARR
DUST

STARR DUST

STARR
DUST

STARR
DUST

BEST FRIENDS

Social-Emotional Learning (S.E.L.) Connection:

Try It YourS.E.L.f!

Have you ever regretted a rash decision or an unkind or impulsive response like Starr and Sunny? Our "downstairs brain" can make us act before we think! Moving into our "upstairs brain" helps us to think before we act!

Five Steps for Moving Up:

1. Be calm and breathe.

2. Notice and name your feelings.

3. When your big emotions have settled, think about strategies you already know for solving problems and responding appropriately.

4. Consider what strategy you could apply to make a good decision in the situation you're currently facing.

5. Take positive action and congratulate yourself!

☆ READING GUIDE ☆

Talk It Over With Your Shiny Friends!

This story is told from two characters' points of view. How is this helpful for understanding perspective?

Is there an event in the book that you'd like to see from another character's perspective? Why?

If you could step into the story, what would you do to help solve the conflict? Write that scene with yourself in it!

Do any of the characters in the story remind you of yourself or someone else you know? How so?

Why do you think the author wrote this book? What was her purpose?

Who is your favorite character? What would you talk about together at the lunch table?

In this book, both Starr and Sunny do things they regret, and both of them try to make things right. Can you relate?

If you could choose a different event from the book to put on the cover, what would it be? Sketch it, and explain your design.

Did you learn anything from the story that you can use in real life?

What is your favorite part? Why?

Meet the Author

For Leigh Reagan Alley, the 4th-great-granddaughter of Maine folk hero Tall Barney Beal, tall tales are part of her family's DNA! Raised in a Downeast lobstering village where storytelling tradition is alive and well, and trained to be a writer and educator in Maine universities that she still serves today, Leigh teaches children's and young adult literature in the University of Maine System where she is an Assistant Professor of Education. Her lobstering husband and their two lobstering children are her three favorite people to share stories with.

Meet the Illustrator

Mark Nathan Hurry studied art and design at Newcastle College, earning himself a diploma before going to university where he received his bachelor's degree in illustration. Mark is a collector of children's literature and has made picture books specially for his daughter who has sensory processing disorder. Residing in Newcastle upon Tyne, England, with his three beautiful girls, his wife, cat, and dog, it is life with them that inspires his work.

Printed in Great Britain
by Amazon

40343517R00079